Better Homes and Gardens

Professional Sewing Tips

Better Homes and Gardens Books

New York   **Des Moines**

BETTER HOMES AND GARDENS CREATIVE SEWING LIBRARY, SECOND PRINTING

©MEREDITH CORPORATION, 1966. ALL RIGHTS RESERVED

PRINTED IN THE UNITED STATES OF AMERICA

SBN: 696-01201-4

CREATIVE SEWING

Beautiful fabrics and exciting pattern styles make sewing more rewarding than ever. With today's new techniques and equipment, sewing can be fun for the beginner as well as the accomplished seamstress.

Better Homes and Gardens Creative Sewing Library presents sewing methods based on common sense— practical, professional tips that show how to give clothes for the whole family a "custom-made" look.

The Creative Sewing Library has been prepared under the guidance of Miss Lucille Rivers, one of America's eminent sewing experts. To help women learn the easy, professional methods of sewing she describes in the books, she has drawn upon her long experience in the field. Miss Rivers has directed her own custom salon in New York, and she has served as consultant to many leading clothing manufacturers.

She has created new styles for fashion shows, and has lectured on sewing in department stores in this country, Australia, and New Zealand. For many years Miss Rivers was sewing editor of NBC's popular "Home Show," and she has conducted sewing demonstrations on many other television programs. In the Creative Sewing Library, she shares her fashion knowledge and dressmaking experience with you.

Titles in the Creative Sewing Library are:
Professional Sewing Tips
How to Sew for Children
Pattern Adjustments
Tailoring Suits and Coats
Sewing Casual Clothes

CONTENTS

Easy sewing methods

There are "tricks to every trade," and the sewing trade is no exception! Short cuts and newer methods are constantly being developed to speed up and improve workmanship.

These same professional methods can be a help to home sewers. Too often, it is the finishing touches on a garment that make it look "home-made."

A poorly made buttonhole, a badly rolled collar, corners that aren't quite square—all detract from the quality appearance of clothes, and give them that "loving-hands-at-home" look.

Professionally made clothing has a look of quality because the detail is so beautifully finished. And, these professional tricks are easier and faster than many of the old methods learned at home.

On the following pages you'll learn how to use professional techniques for making cord-bound buttonholes, and for collars that roll as beautifully as those on expensive ready-to-wear.

There are tips on sewing curved insets, making sharp angle corners, and using facings and interfacings. You'll also learn how to make perfect bias bindings, cording, and tubing.

The bound buttonhole is an example of these easier, faster methods. A dozen ways of making it are taught in home sewing classes. None are too accurate, and all require long practice. In the sewing trade, only one type of bound buttonhole is used— the cord-bound buttonhole. It is easy and foolproof to make. The cord-bound buttonhole can be used on all fabrics, except sheers where a bound buttonhole is never used.

It is easy to do the finishing details before you assemble the garment. If it opens down the front, you will want to make the buttonholes before you join the waistline or finish the neck. In the future, you can make the buttonholes before the garment is even assembled for a try-on.

Cord-bound buttonhole

Have the actual button you are going to use on hand before you start your buttonhole. With the following method of marking, you can use any size button, and as many of them as you like. If you want more buttons than indicated on the pattern, it's no trick to mark and place them.

Be sure you measure your buttons accurately to make sure the buttonholes are the correct size.

Flat buttons: Measure across the top. Make your buttonhole the diameter of the button, plus 1/8 inch.

Thick, chunky buttons: Measure by cutting a slash in a scrap of fabric. Slide the button through the slash. When it goes through easily, measure the slash for the size of buttonhole. Nonwoven fabric is good to use for measuring, since it won't stretch. A slightly larger buttonhole will wear better than one that is too small.

Making the cording

To make the cording for the buttonholes, cut a strip of true bias 1¼ inches wide from your dress fabric. (If you are short of fabric, use small scrap pieces of fabric 1 inch longer than the buttonholes. Be sure pieces are on the true bias.)

Fold the bias piece over cable cord that is 1/8 inch in diameter, or over No. 9 cord, and stitch by machine close to the cord. Use the cording foot on your sewing machine, and stretch the bias slightly as you sew. It's important to do this carefully because this covered cord forms the lip of the cord-bound buttonhole.

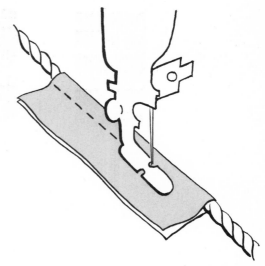

Adjust the cording foot on your machine correctly before you sew the bias. Line up the needle with the cut-out edges on the right side of cording foot.

Always use the same size cording. If the fabric you have chosen is heavy, the cording will automatically be heavier after it is covered. It adjusts itself to the fabric weight you are using.

Here's an easy trick that's most helpful. If you're sewing on a dark fabric where self-colored stitching is difficult to see, stitch the cording with a bright-colored thread.

It won't show on the finished buttonhole, and will be easier to see against the fabric when you sew the pieces of cord to the garment.

Measure for placement of buttonholes

Take the pattern piece marked for

the buttonholes, and make a tissue paper tracing of it.

The finished tissue tracing will look exactly like a facing piece.

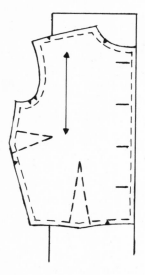

Next, check the original pattern piece for the center front line—or the line where the buttonholes start.

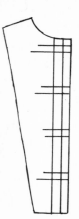

Use a ruler to draw a vertical line on the tracing paper at this point. Measure in from this line the exact width of the buttonholes, and draw a second vertical line. You'll have two vertical lines running parallel to each other.

Across the two vertical lines, draw two horizontal lines to show exact placement of each buttonhole. Distance between the two horizontal lines should be equal to four thicknesses of the covered cording.

Then fold the covered cord as illustrated in the drawing at right above, and measure. The weight of the fabric will affect the width of this space.

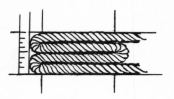

Four thicknesses of the covered cording divide the two horizontal lines.

If the garment you are making has an attached facing, carefully press it back, making a fold line.

Now your tissue pattern is ready to use. Pin it firmly in position on the *right side* of your dress.

When you sew the cording in place, you'll stitch through the tissue paper pattern and the garment front, but not through the facing. Pin the tissue tracing from the fold line.

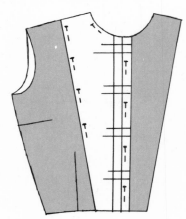

To prevent raveling, use an interfacing under the buttonholes. A lightweight, nonwoven type is best. Pin the interfacing to the wrong side of the dress under buttonhole markings.

Put the regular sewing foot back on your machine before you sew the cording in place. (If you have a zigzag sewing machine, do *not* use the wide zigzag foot; use the narrow, straight-stitching machine foot.)

Sew cording in place

First, cut the cording into lengths 1 inch longer than the buttonholes. Sew the first strip of cording with the fold edge along the upper line of the buttonhole, and the seam allowance toward the center. Sew from one vertical line to the other. The cording should extend ½ inch on either side of the buttonhole. If your sewing machine sews backward, sew back and forth a few stitches at either end of the cording to make it secure.

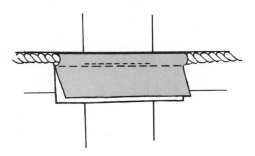

Sew the second strip of cord along the lower line of the buttonhole, with seam allowance toward the center. *Don't cut off the seam allowance.* It makes the buttonhole easier to work, and can be trimmed away later. Sew inside the stitching line when sewing

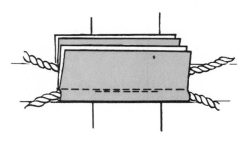

on the cording. The buttonhole will be finer and the stitching won't show. Contrasting thread used to sew the bias on the cord will help you stitch the cord correctly in place.

Stitch cording to all the buttonhole marks at once. Turn the dress to the wrong side and check stitching lines of buttonholes. Make sure all stitching lines are the same length and are spaced the same width apart.

If the lengths of stitching lines aren't equal, it's easy to rip out a few stitches to correct them. If stitching lines aren't the same distance apart, however, rip out incorrect cording, restitch correctly.

Rip out uneven stitches

Stitching even

If stitching lines are wider apart than width of two cords, your buttonhole will have too wide a space between lips. Correct by removing one cord, restitching closer together.

When all your buttonhole lines are correctly stitched, tear off the tissue pattern. Then, on the wrong side, slash through the center of each buttonhole to about ¼ inch from each end. Next, slash diagonally into the corner of each buttonhole.

This is a vital place in the making of the buttonhole. These ends are used in finishing it, so be sure to cut them carefully. Then turn the cording to the inside of the garment, and the cords will automatically form the lip of the buttonhole.

Slashed center

Diagonal slashes

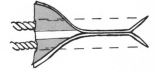

Finishing the buttonhole

Fold the garment out of the way and stitch the small extended point, formed when you cut into the corners of each buttonhole, to the cording (A). Keep the cords close together when sewing the point. Sew back and forth a few times to make the point secure and to square the corners (B).

As you sew across the points, make sure the interfacing is caught in.

To finish the back of the buttonhole, sew as you do for any bound buttonhole (C). See the section on "Finishing Buttonholes," page 37.

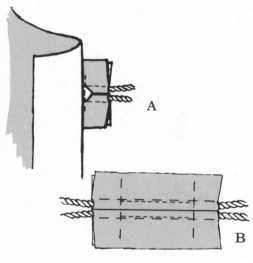

A

B

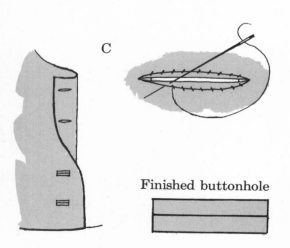

C

Finished buttonhole

Peter Pan collar

The collar is a prominent part of any garment. Use this professional trick to prevent the curling edges of a "dog-eared" collar.

Roll and shape the collar before it is sewed to the dress.

This type of collar is usually interfaced; choose the interfacing to suit the dress fabric. On cottons, for instance, you might use organdy, batiste, lawn, or a commercial woven or nonwoven type of interfacing.

There are slight differences in the way nonwoven and woven interfacings are used for collars.

Nonwoven interfacing

Cut the upper and under collar and the interfacing from the pattern piece. Trim away the seam allowance

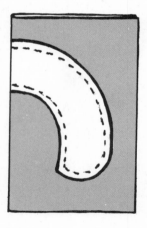

on the outside edges of the interfacing except at the neckline. Do this because nonwoven interfacing fabrics are crease-resistant and, if sewed into the seam, cannot be pressed to give a fine, sharp edge around the collar. Place the nonwoven interfacing against the wrong side of the under collar and stitch it carefully into its proper position. The stitching used at this point should be placed

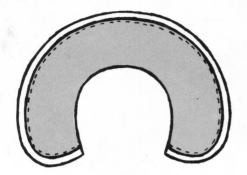

very close to the edge of the nonwoven interfacing. Since it is firm and won't ravel, the edge acts as a guideline, as well as permanently insuring a uniform shape to the collar.

To make the collar roll correctly, always make the upper collar slightly larger than the under collar. On suits, the pattern usually makes this

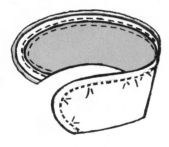

allowance. On dresses, collars are cut from the same pattern piece, so it is necessary for you to make the proper allowance on the upper collar.

The amount of difference in size depends on the weight of the fabric. If you bring the upper collar in $\frac{1}{8}$ inch from the edge of the under collar, it should provide enough ease for the collar to roll correctly in an average weight fabric. On a heavier fabric, it may be necessary to allow slightly more ease in the collar.

As you pin the collars together, ease the upper collar slightly all around. This ease provides enough

space for the upper collar to roll over the under collar and interfacing.

If you are sure of the amount to trim, you can cut the under collar smaller before sewing the collars together this way. The ease will then be allowed in the upper collar before collars are pinned together.

Here's another professional trick. When you trim the seam allowance, graduate the seam widths; trim the upper collar seam allowance about $\frac{1}{4}$

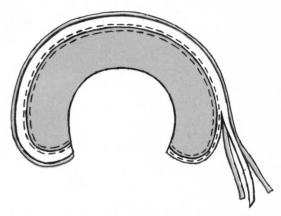

inch, and the under collar seam allowance only half that amount. This makes the edge of the collar more flat. Clip the seam every $\frac{1}{4}$ inch all around the curve of the collar before you turn the collar to the right side.

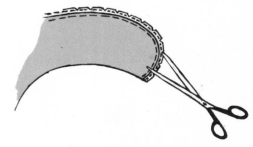

This will make the outside edge of the collar lie smooth and even.

When using a nonwoven interfacing, you can usually press around the collar without basting. Otherwise, baste all around before pressing.

Always bring the seamline back

slightly on the underside so a fold edge is along the outside edge of the collar. The collar edge will then easily press flat and smooth.

Now use this professional trick. Place the right side of the collar face down on a table. Roll it back over

your hand and pin the edges together at the neckline. The upper collar seam allowance will usually be a little short at the neck edge.

If the collar rolls right, however, this is not important. Just stitch the three thicknesses together at the seamline, regardless of where the upper collar edge comes. The correct roll is now permanently in the collar before it is even sewed to the dress.

Woven interfacing

When you use a woven interfacing, it is not necessary to cut away the seam allowance before it is sewed to under collar. Otherwise, follow the same instructions as for making a shaped collar with nonwoven interfacing.

Cuffs are made and permanently rolled in the same manner before they are sewed to the sleeves.

Applying the collar

Even though you've made a collar

that rolls correctly, you must use care in sewing it to the neckline. A professional tip will help you sew the collar in place easily.

First, mark the center back of the collar and neckline with a short clip mark, as you do for notches. Starting at the center front, pin the collar in place all around the neck. Match the neckline notches and the center back marks. After the collar is pinned you can then sew it in place.

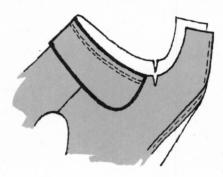

It's easier to pin and sew only the collar itself first; the facings can be pinned and sewed afterward. Don't try to pin the collar and facing pieces at the same time.

At this point, the professional sewer checks the collar again. When the collar is pinned on, it is eased slightly all around the neck.

Usually, you sew on a collar from the left side of the neck around to the right side, and there is a tendency for the ease to shift slightly as you sew. Unless you are careful, you may find all the ease has shifted to the right side of the collar. This will make the left side look shorter.

RIGHT　　　　WRONG

To prevent this, sew from the center toward the right. Then start at the center again and sew toward the left side. This will keep the ease from shifting to one side.

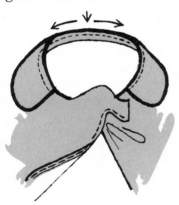

All shaped collars can be made in the same general way as the Peter Pan collar. Use the same technique for any size collar you make.

There are, however, various ways the collar can be applied, depending on the dress style you choose.

When the Peter Pan collar is used on a *one-piece front*, it is important that the collar meet in front and that the ends be the same length.

Bring the front edges of the collar

together. Stitch about an inch on either side of the front edges on the seam allowance line. This holds the front edges in place before sewing the collar to the dress.

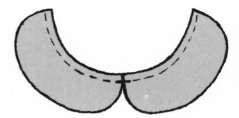

On some styles, the collar extends to the edge of the front opening.

It's difficult to make the collar line up with the front edge of the dress unless you use this simple trick. If an attached facing that folds back is used, slash down on the fold edge of the facing to the seam allowance line. As you pin the collar to the neck, the front corner of the collar

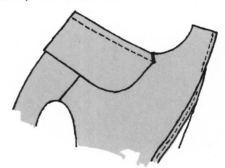

seam allowance will extend through this slash. This brings the seam allowance lines of both the collar and neckline together at the point where they should be sewed to form a smooth front line from the collar to the neck opening.

When a stitched-on facing is used, the neckline seam is left open to the seam allowance line so the collar can be applied in the same way.

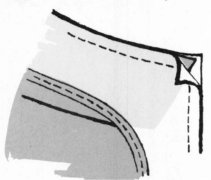

V neck with a collar

This type of collar (a sailor collar, for instance) is also fairly difficult to apply. The front edges should always come together at the exact center of the front point.

To accomplish this, measure and mark the seam allowance at the front

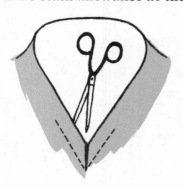

V of the neck. Stitch on this line for 2 inches on either side of the point. Stitching can be done in contrasting thread. Slash down to the stitching line at this point. When you pin the collar in place, the front edges of the collar will slide through this slash, and the seam allowance line of the

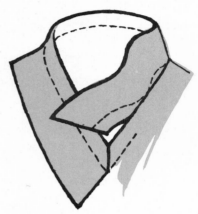

collar will be pinned at the end point of the slash.

Stitch the collar to the neck of the dress to hold it in place before you apply the facing. Pin the facing so that the collar is between the facing

and the front. Sew them together from the bodice side. At the point, sew just outside of the original stitching line which holds the collar. Clip the facing to the depth of the V in front before turning it to the inside. Trim and clip the seam.

Angle corners— curved insets

Angle corners

Many construction details—corners and angle joinings, for example—require the same general sewing method. Learn to make these details correctly and use the same method for many styles. Sketches at right show similar constructions.

For some reason, sewing two pieces of fabric together to form a corner seems to cause trouble for the average sewer. Corners are not sharp and clear, or they start to fray before they are even sewed. If you follow the pattern seam allowance carefully, you can avoid these problems.

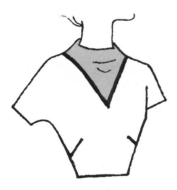

It is usually the seam allowance at a corner that is confusing, because of the degree of the angle. Here's a professional method that solves all the problems. On the pieces to be joined, measure and mark the seam allowances for 2 inches from either side of the corner. Use a ruler to measure accurately.

At the right angle to the seam, measure in the amount of the seam allowance ($\frac{5}{8}$ inch, unless the pattern specifies otherwise).

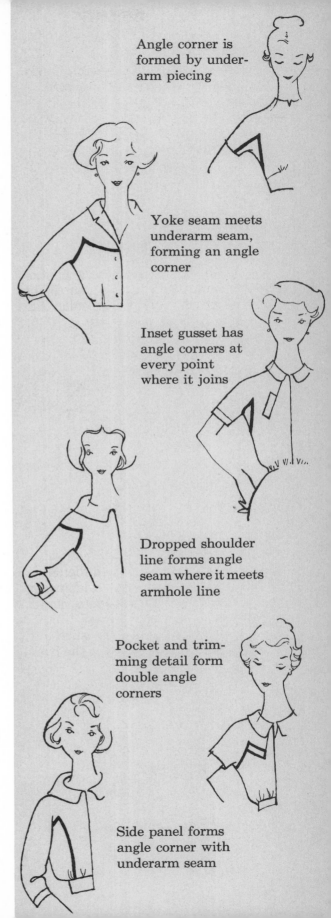

Angle corner is formed by underarm piecing

Yoke seam meets underarm seam, forming an angle corner

Inset gusset has angle corners at every point where it joins

Dropped shoulder line forms angle seam where it meets armhole line

Pocket and trimming detail form double angle corners

Side panel forms angle corner with underarm seam

Using a ruler, draw a chalk line on this mark, parallel to the seam edge. Now measure and mark the other angle of the corner. Stitch along these lines for 2 inches on either side of the corner. Use thread in a con-

trasting color. Now clip into the corner as close to the stitching as possible without cutting through the stitches. The slash will be much deeper than the seam allowance because you've cut at an angle. Sometimes it will be as much as 1 inch in depth. A common mistake is to slash into the corner only $5/8$ inch, instead

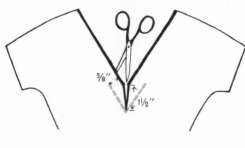

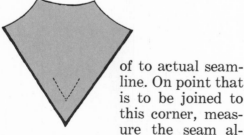

of to actual seam-line. On point that is to be joined to this corner, measure the seam allowance and mark it with chalk. Stitch on this line for 2 inches at either side of the point—again in thread of a contrasting color so it will show against the fabric.

The base of the slash should be at the point of the stitched seam allowance line on the piece to be inserted. Pin the rest of the seam at one side of the slash mark. Always pin and sew the seams with slash side up.

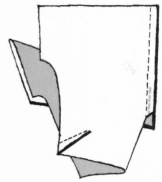

Now swing the slash open and pin the seams together at the other side of the angle. When you start to sew

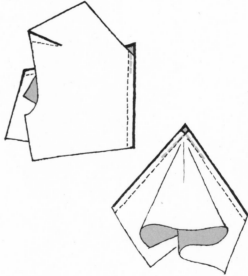

the pieces together, stitch just inside the original stitching line on both pieces for a perfect corner.

When sewing a corner, reinforce it with an underfacing to prevent raveling, especially if the fabric is soft or loosely woven. A nonwoven underlining is best; the bias finish is soft enough to be used under any weight of fabric. Cut a small piece and sew it in the corner as you do the stitching for seamline. Keep underfacing flat along inside of dress as you stitch.

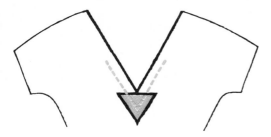

When you join for the point, sew it in with the regular seam.

Many other points on your clothes will also have to be marked and sewed like this. For instance, the shawl collar is done in the same way.

Shawl collar

Mark and stitch seam allowance 2 inches in each direction from the point at which the neck and shoulder seams meet on the bodice back.

Do the same on the corner of collar and the facing. You can stitch with thread of a contrasting color, which is easier to see and will not show on the finished side. After the corner has

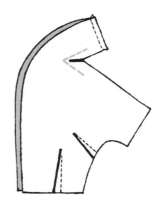

been stitched, clip in at an angle to this stitching line.

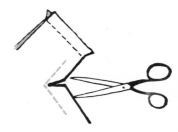

Pin the front and back shoulder seams together. The base of the slash on the front shoulder should meet the point on the back shoulder and neck.

The slash spreads open as the collar is pinned to the back neckline.

Stitch within the original stitching line when you join the back and front bodice pieces at this corner. When stitched in this way, the neck and shoulder will fit correctly, and the corners will be sharp and clear.

Gussets

Here's another construction detail based on the same principle. Treat the slash end of the gusset in the same manner as you do a corner.

Mark the slash line carefully from your pattern. Then, cut a piece of material 1½ by 3 inches; use any lightweight, firm interfacing, preferably of the nonwoven type.

Place this piece of fabric on the underside of the garment at the end of the slash line. Catch the piece in

place as you sew the line of stitching that reinforces the corner.

As you sew, carefully follow the lines marked from the pattern. The angle of these lines is important. As you come to the end of the slash line, take one extra stitch across the end before sewing the other side of the slash. Mark the seam allowance at the points of the gusset pieces and stitch for 1 inch on either side. Stitch in thread of a contrasting color, which is easier to see.

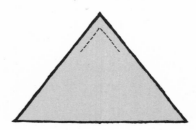

Now, with right sides together, pin the gusset into the slash. Start at the end of the slash and pin it to the point of the gusset.

Stitching lines of contrasting colored thread on each of these pieces will serve as guidelines.

Pin one side of the slash to one side of the gusset piece; spread the other side of the slash open and pin it to the other side of the gusset. Take a

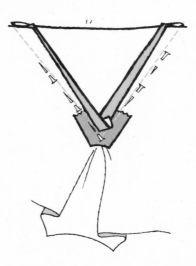

full ⅝-inch seam on the gusset as you sew the pieces together. The seam allowance on the slash is ⅝ inch at the opening, tapering to nothing at the end. This is why the stitching is needed as a guideline and for reinforcement at this delicate corner on an angle joining of this type.

Curved insets

This curved detail should always have a clean, clearly defined outline. Again, an easy, professional trick will assure good results.

After you clip all the notches for matching, remove the pattern from

the pieces to be joined. Before sewing the curved seams together, run a machine-stitch along the seam allowance lines of the individual pieces. On the inside curved seam, clip into this stitching line every ½ inch. Pin

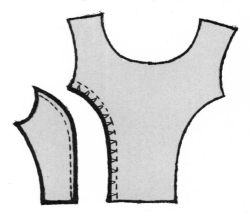

seam together with the clipped seam on the top. Keep the edges of both seams even. Stitch just inside the original stitching line when sewing the seams together, and you'll have a firm, perfectly shaped seam.

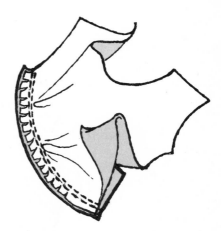

There is a tendency for this type of seam to stretch and ripple unless it is sewed on the inside first. Patterns often suggest outside stitching on the yoke or curved seam edges as a trim. Always sew the seam on the inside first. Do trimming stitch after you have pressed the seam.

Turning a corner

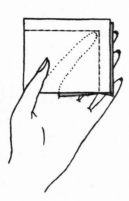

This is the professional way to turn a corner; it eliminates a thick, lumpy look, makes corner lie flat.

Turn the fabric wrong side out; insert your first finger into the corner between the two layers of fabric, under side of your finger turned up toward you.

Turn down one seam allowance toward you along the stitching line. Hold in place with the thumb. Then turn the other seam allowance toward you along the stitching line. Also hold this with the thumb. Press-

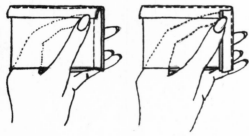

ing the seam allowances between thumb and first finger, turn the corner to the right side. The corner will be flat and smooth because you have held the seam allowances in place on the inside. They stay flat, instead of lumping or rolling, as they do if just turned and prodded into place with a pointed instrument.

If the fabric is a little bulky, you can eliminate some thickness by cutting one layer of fabric away diagonally across corner. Hold cut layer toward you as you turn corner.

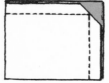

Facings

It's advisable to interface a dress that opens down the front. On the buttonhole side, cut the interfacing like the facing and put it to the wrong side of the front so the buttonholes can be made through it.

If it is a fold-back facing, cut the interfacing only to the fold line. Blind-tack the edges of the interfacing to the dress with a catch-stitch.

If it is a convertible neckline that may be opened, then interface the left side of neck in the same way.

If tacking stitch shows on right side, use only a patch of interfacing under each buttonhole. Sew interfacings to both facings by hand.

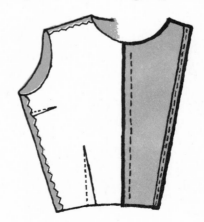

If the fronts close up to the neckline, the interfacings on the left side can be stitched to the facings by machine, then turned to the inside.

If the facings are sewed to the front, interfacings can be sewed into the seam, with the exception of the non-woven type of interfacing.

Children's clothes can be finished with bias at the neck, but in women's garments, a shaped facing is a finer finish. If your pattern doesn't include a shaped facing for the back (or front) of the neck, you can easily cut one from the pattern of the back and front bodice. Sew the facings together at the shoulder. Then turn the outside edge back ¼ inch and sew.

Facings used with a collar

You have already sewed the collar to the neck of your dress. It's only necessary to pin the right side of the facing over the right side of the dress on the seam allowance line and sew to complete this step. The collar is between the two fabric layers and will not slip, since it is already sewed firmly in place.

It isn't necessary to interface the back neck facing when a collar is used. All you need do is trim the seam allowance and then clip around the neck about every ¼ inch.

Facings for other types of necklines

Round neck

Choose the interfacing to suit your dress fabric. Cut facings and interfacings from the same pattern pieces.

If a nonwoven type of interfacing is used, cut away the neck seam allowance on the interfacing.

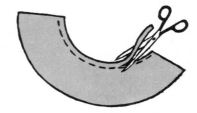

Shoulder seams of the facings and interfacings are sewed separately. Place the interfacing against the wrong side of the facing. The neckline seam allowance will extend all around. Stitch interfacing in place.

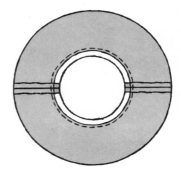

If the fabric ravels, cut ¼ inch off the interfacing at the outside edge, turn upper fabric back and sew.

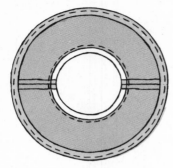

On a firm or heavy fabric, stitch the outside edges together and pink.

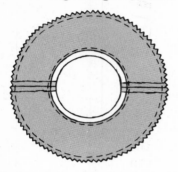

Put the right side of the facing to the right side of the neck and stitch. The trick is to stitch along the edge of the interfacing, not through it. Trim the neckline seam away in graduated widths. Then carefully clip to the stitching line about every ½ inch all around the neckline.

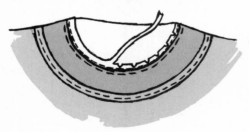

When using any woven fabric as an interfacing, it is not necessary to cut away the seam allowance at the neckline. Sew facings and interfacings together before stitching facings to the dress. Follow the same method in sewing all other details.

Shaped neckline

For this neckline, use only a non-woven interfacing. It helps to achieve and retain the shape of neckline.

Cut interfacing and facing from the same pattern piece. On the interfacing, cut away the neckline seam and design detail to the finished line. Sew it to the facing along the edge.

Nonwoven interfacing will not ravel and acts as a guideline so detail will be perfectly matched. Follow instructions as you do for facing the round neck of a garment.

Square neckline

Cut interfacing and facing from the same pattern piece. Choose the interfacing to suit the upper fabric. On a nonwoven interfacing, cut away the seam allowance at the neckline. Be careful to make a square corner. To

be sure the corners are correct, it's

a good idea to mark the seam allowance at each corner with tailor's chalk. Sew with contrasting thread.

Follow the same instructions as for the round neck when applying the interfacing to facings. As you sew the

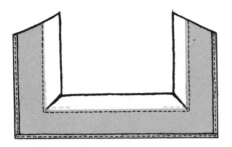

facings to the neck, be sure to follow the stitching marks at each corner for really sharp corners.

Again, graduate neckline seams as you trim them. It's only necessary to clip around the neck at the back where it is curved. Slash well into the corners, all the way to the stitching, for a truly professional look.

Facing the sleeveless dress

The sleeveless dress is popular for dress-up clothes as well as for playtime fashions. Sometimes, the dress top is completely lined.

In many patterns the neck and armholes are faced all in one piece, which is a better finish. The professional method is fast, and can be done entirely by machine.

Sew all of the bodice together, except for the shoulder seams. Also,

sew the facings together, except for the shoulders.

Now put the right side of the facing against the right side of the dress and stitch to 2 inches from the end of the shoulder seam on both the neckline and the armhole.

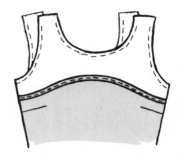

Trim away half of the seam allowance where the neckline and armholes have been faced, and clip the seam all around. Then turn the garment to the right side and press.

Here's the professional trick. Turn the back shoulder strap inside out. Slide the front shoulder strap into

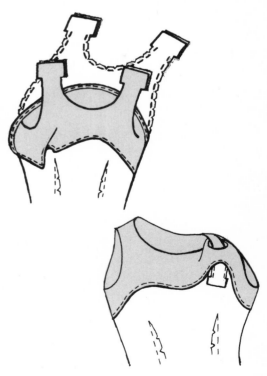

the back strap. The right side of the front will be against the right side of the back. Pin front and back shoulder seams together and sew.

The front and back facing will also come together. Pin them and sew.

Then pull the front even farther

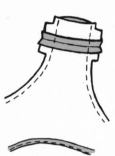

into the back strap, so the openings at the sides of the shoulder straps are clear. Press open the shoulder seams. Stitch the openings on either side, and trim the seam. Pull front shoulder strap into position. This will automatically turn back shoulders to right side.

The entire top of the dress will now be faced, with only minor hand-tacking needed to finish the garment. Follow these same instructions if the top of the dress is to be completely lined in self-fabric.

When the top is to be lined in a China silk or other type of lining, however, the dress and the lining are sewed together—the wrong side of the lining against the wrong side of dress, as when lining a sheath.

Facing pieces are cut of self-fabric and are handled as though the dress were not being lined. This is necessary because soft or contrasting linings have a tendency to roll out and show at the neck edges.

If the dress is lined with a more crisp fabric, like taffeta, the fabric has enough body to serve as a facing. In this case, apply lining to the dress as if it were a facing.

Bias

Bias is made by cutting material on the diagonal grain. This creates a greater elasticity, which permits the bias to be used in more ways than a straight piece of fabric can.

It must be cut on the true bias, however, or it will twist and pull and be difficult to use. Many home sewers find it hard to use bias they make themselves, but have no difficulty with commercial bias. This professional ·trick will help you make a binding from self-fabric that is as easy to use as a commercial binding. Here's how it's done.

Bias binding

To get a true bias, fold material so crosswise thread runs parallel to the lengthwise thread, or selvage. Mark the width you want with chalk. Cut the bias strip twice the finished width, plus ½ inch seam allowance.

Join all bias pieces on the length of the goods. Fold the bias on the

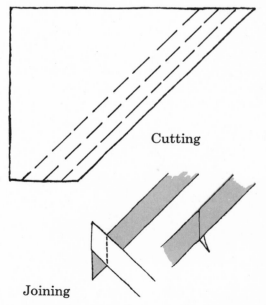

Cutting

Joining

length, press, and stitch. Trim the edges so the entire length of the bias is even. Bias piece is now ready to use. You'll find it as easy to work with as any commercial binding.

Roll binding (French piping)

Used on sheer fabrics or as a trim. Take the pressed binding and sew the raw edges to the edges of the garment, right sides together.

Trim the seam to half the width of the binding and roll the fold edge over it. Tack in place just under the stitching line. When binding is used to finish a round neck, it should stay flat against neck and not ripple. Pin or baste a few inches of binding to neck, stretching it as you go. Roll to test for ripples. If correct, sew to neck, stretching in same way.

Bias facing

For a smooth, flat bias facing, trim one side of the bias off between the fold edge and the raw edge.

If bias is to be used on a curve (around a neck, for example), curve the bias to the shape of the neck with an iron before applying it to garment.

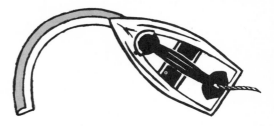

Sew the raw edge to the neckline. The fold edge should be held flat to the neck, as it will be when finished. Trim the neck seam and clip in every $\frac{1}{2}$ inch along the seam to the stitching line. Turn bias to the inside, press, and slip-stitch into place.

This method of making bias binding is quick and easy. It makes an even bias with the outer edge folded and ready to be finished.

Sewing a bias sash

Bias is easy to handle when you press and stretch it to form binding, or when you cut and sew it over cord to form cording. But, try to sew a bias fold of fabric to form a sash, and it seems to twist and turn, no matter how carefully you sew it. Here is a professional trick that will insure a perfect sash, with no twisting.

Place the fold of bias on the ironing board, right side out. Stretch and press it on a fold. While it is stretched on the board, clip the seam at the open edge of the sash every 4 inches for the entire length.

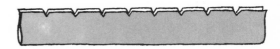

Remove from the board and turn so the right sides are together, ready to sew the seam. As you sew, stretch the seam, matching the clip marks all along the seam allowance. Leave

about 4 inches open in the center of

the seam. Turn to the right side through this opening. Baste along the seamline to hold in place until it is pressed. Press lightly, then remove the basting, and give it a final pressing. Slip-stitch the 4-inch opening together by hand.

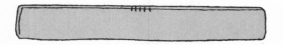

Bias cording—piping

Formerly, bias bindings were used only on children's clothes and aprons. Fashions now feature self-binding and cording on necklines, pockets, and jacket edges. Especially on jackets, self-fabric bindings and cording, as well as braids, are used extensively. Here's a professional tip for handling self-cording.

Cording

Cording is a decorative trim used in seams and around collars. Cut bias and cover the cording as you do for a cord-bound buttonhole. (See page 7.) Generally, the same $\frac{1}{8}$-inch cording is used, so bias should be $1\frac{1}{4}$ inches.

Occasionally, a heavier cording is used for a trim. The bias should then be cut wider. There should always be a $\frac{1}{2}$-inch seam allowance.

If the cording is to be used in the edge of a collar, then clip the cording

seam; sew the cord to the right side, with the seam edges of the collar and the cording even.

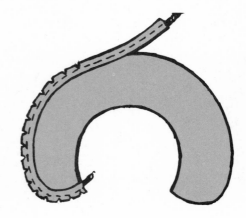

Next, pin the facing directly to the collar with the stitching line of the cording showing on collar side.

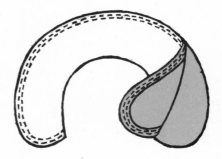

Sew upper and under collars together along this stitching line. Trim the seam. On the round collar, notch it as well. Turn the collar to the right side; cording will be in place, and

seam flat and smooth, neatly in place.

The same method is used for cording the seam of a garment. Sew the cording to the right side first so you can see that it is accurate. Then, permanently join the seams by stitching along the original cord stitching line on the wrong side.

Corded piping and facing

When a cording is used around neck, armhole, or sleeve, you can use the bias of the cording as the finish, rather than a separate facing.

Cut the bias about 3 inches wide. Press this bias strip in half on the length. Then cut away one side of it as you do for bias facing. Leave a ½-inch turn-back. Fold the other edge over the cording and sew the cording in place where indicated.

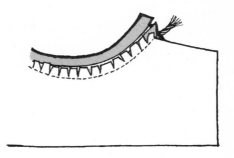

Put this side face down on the right side of the dress and sew. The bias will extend well beyond the seam edge of the dress. If the binding is

used on a curved seam, such as the neck, this seam must be clipped all around as you do on any curve.

Turn the bias to the inside and press. You'll have a corded edge on the garment, with a deep bias facing

that is ready to be tacked in place. If the cording is to be used on a

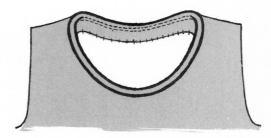

curved seam, such as a neckline, ease the bias piece enough so that it will follow the curve of the neck. Steam press it so that any fullness is smoothed. When the bias is sewed and turned to the inside of the garment, it makes a smooth, flat facing.

Bias rolled neckline

This type of neckline is popular on lightweight jackets and coats. It is made of bias cording, but in a completely different way than the cording shown on page 26.

This cording must be soft, but firm. Cable cord thick enough to give the size of cording needed would be too stiff and hard. The size of the cording can, however, be formed around a suitable size cable cord.

Cut the bias 4 inches wide. The length will depend on size of the neckline, plus the knot and ends. Use 1-inch cable cord; cut it to the finished size of neck, plus tie end and enough extra for the knot.

Mark the finished neck size by clipping. Fold the bias over the cord, wrong side out. Sew bias around the cable cord to neck marks. Leave unstitched at these points. Stitch the other end over the cord. Pull cording out of the bias, and turn bias tube right side out. Pin open edges to the neckline and sew in place. Finish

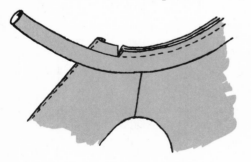

with a facing. Fill the bias cord with strands of 4-ply knitting yarn. Meas-

ure the length of the bias piece. Cut about 15 strands of yarn for filler to double the length of the bias. Fold in half. Tie a cord to the fold and then pull the strands through the bias.

Cut yarn ½ inch shorter than the bias at either end. Turn in the seam allowance at either end and slip-stitch by hand. Here's a professional tip to help you do it easily and correctly. As you sew ends of the bias, ease them in slightly so the ends will look the same size as the cording, rather than forming an unattractive, spatula-shaped, flat end.

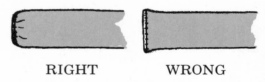

RIGHT   WRONG

Commercial binding

Innumerable types of bindings, in wool, silk, rayon, and cotton, are available. They are woven like military braids, or cut, folded, and pressed of actual bias fabrics. There is a wide range of colors. Some bindings are woven in several colors and serve as a decorative trim. Most of these bindings are folded, ready to apply. They can be sewed entirely by machine-stitching, or partly by machine and finished by hand.

Slide the binding over the edge of the garment. Start to baste along the edge, catching both edges of the binding at one time.

At points around which the binding

requires mitering, this professional trick makes it easy to apply.

If you are binding the front and neckline, sew the binding to the extreme end of the front edge before

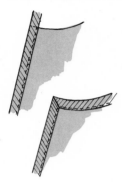

you turn the corner. Sew across the end, holding the two layers of binding together at the top edge of garment. Stretch the binding a little, and begin binding around the neck.

At the corner, fold the binding so corners miter. Mold and shape binding around the neck, basting it into place. Follow the same method on the other side of the neck. Press the binding very lightly, then stitch by machine all along the binding edge.

In some cases where there is a rolled lapel, it is better to sew one side by machine and finish the other by hand. In this case, baste just one side of the binding to the right side of the garment you're making.

To be sure it is put on evenly, keep the fold along the edge of the

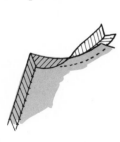

garment, and then baste one side all around. Use the instructions shown above at corners. Do first stitching by machine, and then finish inside by hand.

Self-fabric binding

This binding is beautiful as well as decorative. It is not difficult to make, if you press and shape it before it is applied to the garment.

Cut the bias twice the width of the finished binding, plus double seam allowances. Press it in half on the length. Fold back the seam allowance on the double fold and press. Stretch

it as you press. Open the pressed binding. The creased line of the seam allowance is stitched to the right side of the garment. If the binding is $5/8$ inch wide, stitch it about $1/2$ inch from the garment edge.

Fold over the edge of the garment to the inside and tack the second fold edge to the inside. When a garment has a pointed lapel or neck, the bias must be mitered. Lay the bias on the garment as it will be sewed. Fold and press the miter at the outside corners, actually shaping it to the garment as it will be applied.

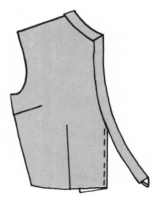

Open the bias to the wrong side. A crease line will now appear where the miter was pressed.

Stitch on this crease line to the folded seam allowance line to finish the miter. Finally, trim away the ex-

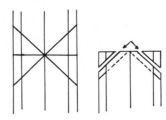

cess seam allowance before turning.

The garment can be bound with the pressed and shaped self-fabric binding, and you will have a perfect miter at the point. The miter is shaped to the inside corner and then

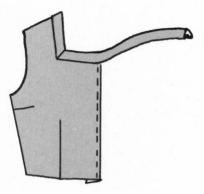

Open the bias. Crease lines will show on the inside. Stitch along these lines to the seam allowance fold line. Next, trim as shown below. Turn, and you have a perfect miter for the inside corner.

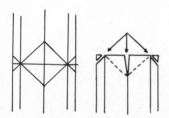

Finish sleeve edges with bias, too. It can be made either way, all by machine, or first stitched by machine and finished by hand-stitching.

Tubing (or "spaghetti")

Tubing, or "spaghetti," is used for frogs, loops, belts, and many other decorative trimmings. There are several types of tubing you can make for different uses.

Plain tubing is soft and pliable, and is used for spaghetti trim. It can

be any thickness. It is made over cable cord, so get the weight of cord that will give you the thickness you want for your design detail. Cut the bias the length you want, making sure it is wide enough to cover the

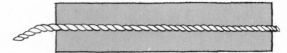

cable cord. Cut a piece of cable cord the same length. Fold the bias over the cording and stitch with the cording foot on your machine. Stretch the bias as much as possible. At the end of the cording, sew the bias to the

cord. If you want the tubing to be soft, then cut away the seam allowance close to the seamline.

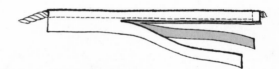

Holding the cord at the open end, slide the bias down over the cord until it turns inside out on itself.

The cording is free and can be cut off. The tubing will be even for the entire length, since cording helped to shape it. Tubing will be soft, however, since it has no filler.

For a firmer tubing, work in the same manner, but leave the seam allowances intact. As the tubing turns inside out, the seam allowance rolls up inside, forming a filler and making it much more firm. Weight of the fabric and the width of the seam will determine the firmness of the tubing.

Corded tubing

Choose the cording thickness you want, and cut the cable cord twice the length of the bias. Fold the bias

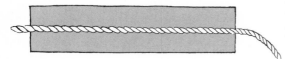

over one end of the cord and sew with a cording foot. Be sure to stretch the bias as you sew. At the end of the bias, sew the bias to the cord. This

will leave about half the cord uncovered. Trim the seam. Draw the

end of the enclosed cord out of the bias. The bias slides down, turning inside out, and automatically covering the other end of the cord.

The exposed end can then be cut away, to leave a firm, corded bias tubing. (See sketch below.)

Pockets

Some pockets are utilitarian, while others are decorative in effect. Learn to make both types so that you can use either style to finish a dress.

Side-seam pockets

These very practical pockets are neatly set in the side seam. You may want to insert them, whether the pattern shows them or not.

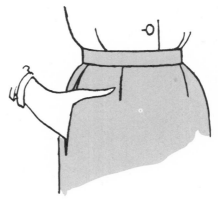

Before the side seams of your skirt have been joined, place the right side of the pocket against the right side of the skirt and sew them together to about 3 inches from the bottom of the pocket or to where it is marked on the pattern.

Clip into the stitching line at the

base of the stitching. Trim the seam. Turn the pocket to the inside.

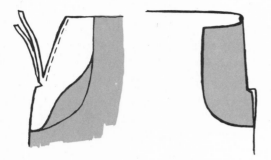

Next, put the right side of the second pocket piece against the front pocket piece and stitch all around.

Stitch the pocket pieces to the front skirt at the base of the pocket on the seam allowance line.

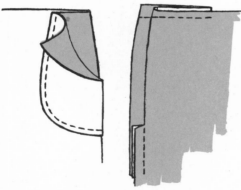

Put the right side of the back and front skirts together and stitch them up the side seam. Stitch on front side of skirt, just inside the line of stitching that holds the pocket pieces in place. Making a side seam pocket is

Slash pocket

This pocket is made with two pieces of fabric, much like the cord buttonhole. (In fact, the corded buttonhole makes a beautiful pocket.)

To make the slash pocket, cut two pieces of fabric 1 inch wide and the length of your pocket, plus seam allowance. Fold the pieces in half on

the length and press. Stitch through the center of each piece. Be sure to have a ¼-inch space on the fold side.

Mark for the placement of the pocket on the dress with a basting thread. Stitch the raw edges of the pocket

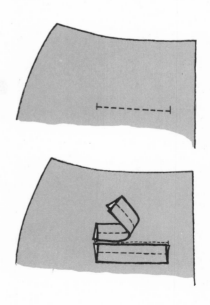

pieces to either side of the basting line to ½ inch from either end. If your dress fabric is soft or ravels easily, reinforce it with an underlining, as you do for buttonholes.

Turn the garment to the wrong side

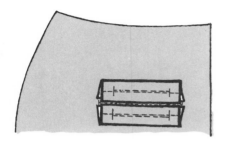

and check the stitching lines. They should be the same length and should be spaced $\frac{1}{2}$ inch apart. If they are uneven, rip the piece and resew it before anything is cut. When stitching lines are even, slash through the center to $\frac{1}{2}$ inch from either end. Then slash diagonally into the corners.

Turn the welt pieces to the inside

to form the pocket. Fold back the dress and stitch the V at each end

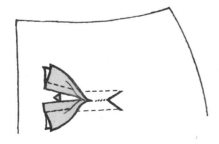

of the pocket to the welt pieces to finish the opening to the pocket.

Now cut out 2 pocket pieces, the

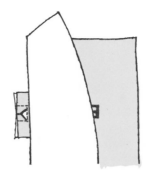

same width as the welts. Decide on the depth of your pocket and make the under pocket $\frac{1}{2}$ inch shorter than the upper pocket. Sew the deeper pocket piece carefully to the upper edge of the welt seam.

Be sure to sew the deeper pocket piece along the original stitching line of the welt, or the upper welt will appear to pucker. The under-pocket piece is stitched to the lower welt. The edge of the pocket piece is along the edge of the lower welt, but it is stitched along the original stitching line of the welt.

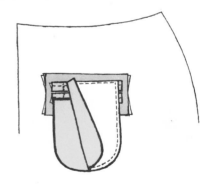

Finish the pocket by stitching its outer edges. Be sure to catch the triangles at either end of the welt

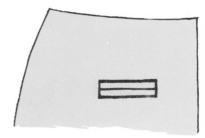

into the seam. The finished pocket will look like a giant buttonhole.

Patch pocket

Before removing pattern, clip on either side for depth of hem. Turn under the seam allowance on the upper edge of the pocket and stitch (A). Turn the hem to the right side of the pocket and stitch along the pocket on the seam allowance line (B).

Clip the seam allowance around the curve of the pocket (C). Turn the hem to the wrong side of the pocket and baste back the seam allowance all around (D). Press the hem, pin the pocket to the dress and then top-stitch edges (E). The pocket can be edge-stitched or sewed about ¼ inch in from edge for trim.

then catch-stitch to the upper flap.

Cut ⅛ inch off lining piece. Pin lining and flap together, keeping edges even. Sew around cut edge of interfacing. Trim seam and clip around curved edge. Turn right side out, baste, and press edge. Top-stitch if patch pocket is finished this way.

The flap can be applied in either of two ways. You can stitch the flap in place ⅝ inch above the pocket, right side of flap to garment. Trim seam ¼ inch. Turn flap down and press. On wrong side of garment, sew underside of flap to garment by hand, just under the trimmed seam.

Using the other method, the flap can be sewed to the garment before applying the pocket. Stitch flap in place along top marking for patch pocket, right side of flap to garment. Stitch the lower edge of flap to garment as well. Pin patch pocket so the upper edge laps the first stitching of flap. Stitch pocket in place. Fold flap down over pocket and press.

Patch pockets can also be sewed by hand, in which case no trim stitch will be needed around the flap.

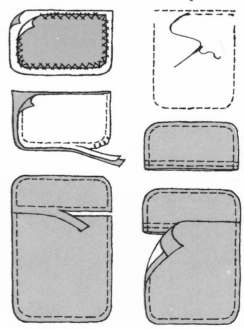

Pocket with flap

A flap is often used with a patch pocket. Line the flap in self-fabric. If it needs body, interface flap. Cut interfacing to finished size of flap and

Finishing details

A dress isn't finished until the last stitch is taken. The way a button is sewed on, or incorrectly tacked facings can make a smart dress look dowdy. Finishing details like these can be easily learned.

Another phase of finishing is not so easily mastered—knowing when and where to use the right detail. For instance, what type button is most suitable? What is the correct hem width for the style of dress and type of fabric you are using? How should certain points on the dress be pressed? Is a self-belt or a ready-made belt more suitable? The answers to these questions depend on your knowledge of sewing—and your good judgment. This book can help increase your skill and knowledge; judgment comes as you gain more sewing experience.

A big mistake many women make is in overdoing the hand finishing. They "nail down" things so tightly that the appearance of the finished garment is ruined. Professionals say that clothes should look "pasted together"; that is, the finishing should be so inconspicuous that it is hardly apparent to the eye.

Save your fine handwork for embroidery or dainty baby garments. It can ruin the appearance of an otherwise beautifully made dress.

Facings

Many types of facings can be used on the bodice. No matter what type of interfacing or finish that you use on a square, V, boat, or round neck, the facings should only be tacked to the neck at a few strategic points.

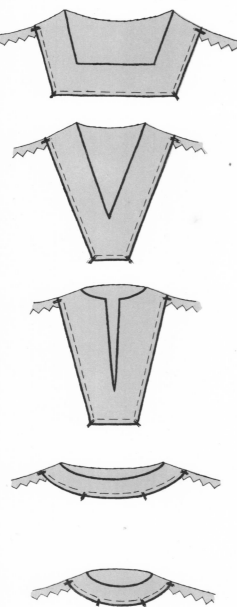

Button-down-front dress

This type of dress, with or without collar, needs little finishing. In fact, tacking the facings down the front of the dress is a sign of the beginner! The only reason for finishing the facings is to hold them firmly to the inside of your dress.

When you finish the buttonholes on one side of the dress and sew the buttons to the other, the facings are automatically held in place. You need only to tack the shoulder seams and a few points at the back of the neck for a neat finish.

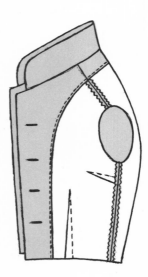

Shawl collar

The facings are usually cut the same as the front of the dress with the back collar attached. This type of neck needs no back facing. The back collar finishes the back neck and also holds the facing in place.

Before the facing is applied to the dress, turn back the inside edge ¼ inch and stitch. Do not turn back the neck and shoulder seam, but clip the corner. To reinforce the corner before clipping, stitch on the seam allowance line for 1 inch on either

Buttonholes and buttons

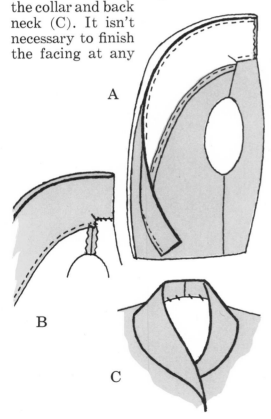

side of the corner. Clip in to this stitching line. Sew the facing (A) to the dress. Trim the seam, then turn it and press. The only finishing needed on this facing is at the shoulder and neck seams (B), which are turned under and tacked into place, finishing the collar and back neck (C). It isn't necessary to finish the facing at any

A

B

C

other points, unless buttons are to be used. Then, of course, the buttonholes and the buttons will hold the facings securely in place down the front of the dress.

Finishing buttonholes

Although the cord-bound buttonhole is easy to make (see page 7), it still must be finished carefully with hand-stitching to avoid puckering the front of the dress.

Fold the facing back to the inside and baste it all around the finished buttonhole, holding the facing and dress front together. Spread the buttonhole from the right side of the garment, and slash facing the length of the buttonhole.

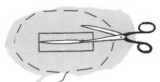

Turn it to the wrong side, and then slash facing to about 1/8 inch longer than the stitching which is at each end of the buttonhole.

Now, turn under this slash edge, and hem the edge to the underside of the buttonhole.

This creates an elliptical shape.

The trick is to turn an extremely fine edge, and not sew it too tightly. Otherwise, your facing will look shrunken, causing the front of the dress to indent along each buttonhole, and the right front will be slightly shorter than the left.

WRONG   RIGHT

Sewing on a button

The entire appearance of a dress can be spoiled by the way a button is sewed on. If the button is sewed too tightly, then the button-hole can't close snugly under it, and the buttonhole spreads, causing the dress front to pucker, the buttons to look as though misplaced.

To sew the button correctly, mark the correct position for it. Remember that the button does not stay in the center of the buttonhole, but slides to the left corner. This is why the left end of the buttonhole starts at the center front line of the garment. Lap the closing and pin it in position. Put a pin through a buttonhole at the left or outer end to mark for the button.

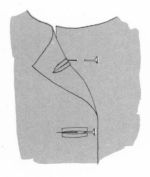

Use a double thread, heavy-duty or buttonhole twist to sew buttons. Take a stitch where the button is to be sewed and then roll the fabric over the index finger (A). With the thumb, hold the button against the fabric, but well away from the button mark. Sew on the button (B). A long stitch will form between the button and the mark on the fabric.

After the button has been sewed, hold it to the end of the long stitch while you wind the thread under it, forming the stem (C). The advantage of this method is that the stem can be made any length needed, depend-

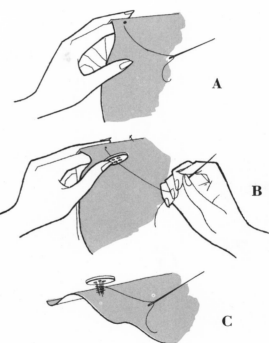

ing on the fabric thickness of the buttonhole that fits around it.

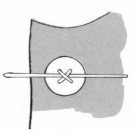

Another method is to take a stitch in the fabric where the button goes. Place a match or a toothpick across the top of the button, and then sew through the holes of the button, joining it to the fabric. After the button has been sewed in place, remove the matchstick and wind the thread around the threads under the button, forming a stem or a shank.

The buttonhole will close tightly around this stem, and the button will ride on top of the buttonhole. This prevents the front from puckering and makes a neat closing.

The shank button, whether metal or self-shank, should also be sewed with a stem. Sew the button very loosely, then wind the thread underneath the button to form the stem. It does not need to be as high as the other type of stem, since the shank itself raises the button.

When a heavy button is used, or a regular button is sewed on one thickness of fabric, it's advisable to use a stay underneath. The stay can be a small button or a piece of fabric. Sew it to the wrong side of the garment as you sew on the button.

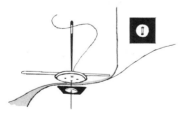

Buttons can also be sewed to form many designs with the thread.

Snaps, hooks and eyes

Sewing on snaps

To sew snap, mark carefully so that socket and ball of snap are placed directly opposite from each other 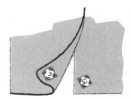 when the joining is correctly lapped. Place the socket side of the snap on the overlap of the garment, the ball part on the underlap. Sew through each hole several times, going under the snap as you sew from hole to hole. Be sure the stitches do not show on the right side of the garment. Fasten the thread securely when the snap is sewed. Be sure the snap is close to the edge you want held in place.

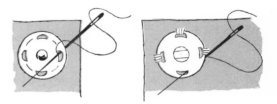

Snaps are useful in many places, but *never* use them down the front of a dress instead of buttonholes.

Learn when to use a snap and when to use a hook and eye. Use the snap when there is no tension; for instance, at the buttoned neckline to hold a corner in place under the collar (A).

A

Use them between widely spaced buttons to keep the front of a garment from bulging (B). Put a snap at the sleeve placket to hold it closed (C). Use it to hold detachable collars and cuffs (D), or to hold the left side of a double-breasted dress in place (E). They are also effective as lingerie strap holders. These are only a few of the places where a snap is the preferred finish—all are points where there is no strain put on the snap.

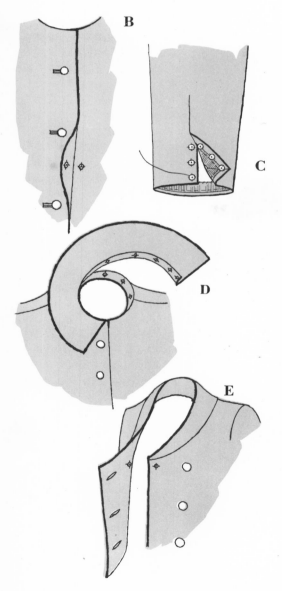

Sewing hooks and eyes

Use hooks and eyes at points where there is strain or tension, or to close some part of a garment inconspicuously. There are two types of eyes. Use the straight, or bar type, when the edges of the garment overlap. Use the round, or loop, eye when the edges come together. Use the same hook with both.

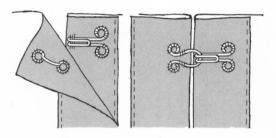

Mark the position for the hook and the eye on the garment. Put the hook on the overlap, or the right-hand side of the closure. Sew the hook about $1/8$ inch from the edge of the garment, using an overcast-stitch to attach the loops of the hook. Then sew a few stitches to hold it firm. Make sure stitches do not show on the right side of the garment. Secure the loops of the eye in the same way. The bar should come just under the bend of the hook when the garment is lapped correctly. When using the round eye, sew it with the loop extending slightly beyond the edge of the garment.

Round eye   Straight eye   Hook

Sometimes a hook and eye is needed on a garment that may be worn open as a jacket. Since the eye will show, make it by hand, using the same color thread as for the garment.

Sew two strands of thread on the underlap where the eye is to go. Cover the strands with a blanket-stitch, made by bringing the needle under the strands and through the loop

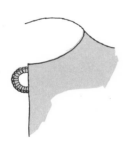

formed. This type of a handmade eye can also be used at the top of a back neck opening. Use the straight eye in the following places: at the waistband of the skirt (A), waistline of coat dress (B), and on inside waistband of dress (C).

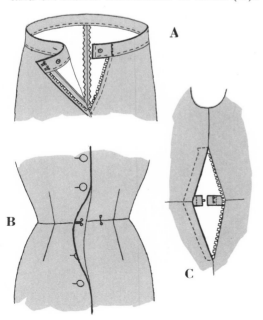

Finishing sleeves

Before setting the sleeves into the finished bodice, it's a good idea to finish them completely. There are as many types of sleeves as there are styles of dresses, but the sewing tricks presented here may be applied, in one way or another, to any sleeve that you decide to make.

Sleeves may be raglan, kimono, or set-in, but all come in only three lengths—short, three-quarter, and long. Each type of sleeve requires different finishing details.

Finishing the short sleeve

When the short sleeve is cut with allowance for the hem, there are two ways it can be finished. First, sew up the underarm seam and press. Then turn under the hem and press.

On washable fabrics, turn under $\frac{1}{4}$ inch on the hem edge and stitch. Slip-stitch the hem to the sleeve.

For other fabrics, sew a seam binding to the edge of the hem and slip-stitch to the sleeve. (Make hem same way on a three-quarter sleeve.)

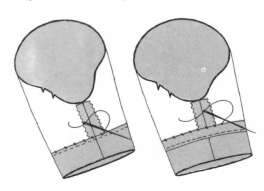

Sleeve facings

Often, the short sleeve is shaped so

that it must be faced. Usually, a shaped facing is included in the pattern, although sometimes a bias facing is recommended instead.

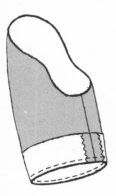

When a shaped facing is used, sew up the underarm seam of the sleeve and the facing.

Press the seams open. Pin the right side of the facing to the right side of the sleeve. Here is the trick: To fit correctly and be smooth, the facing should be slightly smaller than the sleeve. Take the facing in, if necessary, and then ease the sleeve, as you sew facing and sleeve together. Turn facing to inside, and bring it back a small amount so a fold is at the sleeve edge, rather than the seam. Baste around the edge. Press. Turn under edge of facing ¼ inch, stitch. On heavy fabric, sew seam binding to facing edge to finish.

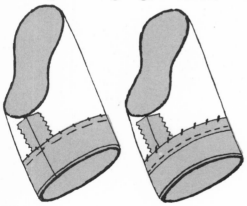

Bias facing

Cut the bias facing about 2 inches wide, and shape it slightly with the iron. Starting at the underarm seam of the sleeve, pin the bias to the sleeve edge. Cut the bias the size of the sleeve, plus seam allowances.

Join the bias on the straight grain. Sew the bias to the sleeve edge, turn to the inside, press. Turn under and stitch a ¼-inch seam at the edge of the bias and slip-stitch to the sleeve.

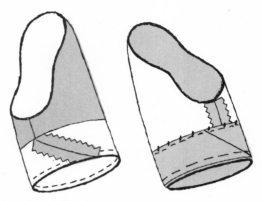

On a heavy fabric, the facings can be cut from a different fabric so the finish will not be too bulky. Taffeta is an excellent choice. On a soft or stretchy fabric, you can interface the shaped sleeve facings just as you do the neckline. The same type of interfacing is generally used for both. (The same facings can be used on the three-quarter sleeve.)

Applying cuffs

On the short sleeve, cuffs are usually made separately, then applied to the sleeve, with a shaped facing, a bias facing, or a self-finish.

Making the two-piece cuff

Cut the upper and under cuff pieces. Then, from the same pattern, cut the interfacing. If a nonwoven type is

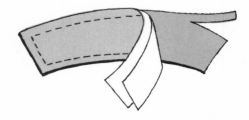

used, cut off the seam allowance on the outside edge. Sew the underarm seams of each cuff piece, making the upper cuff slightly larger, and press open. Lap interfacing seam, stitch, and trim. Pin the interfacing to the under cuff and stitch. Lower edges will be even. The upper edge of the interfacing will be at the seam allowance line. Pin right sides of the cuff pieces together, with the upper cuff on the outside. Sew on the under-cuff side along the edge of the interfacing. (Nonwoven interfacing is not sewed into the seam.)

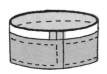
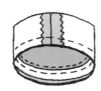

Trim the seam allowance to graduated widths. Turn the cuff to the

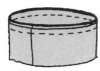

right side. Baste, bringing the under cuff in a bit from the edge, press. Then roll the cuff back with upper cuff on the outside as it will be applied to sleeve.

Since the upper cuff has to roll over the interfacing and under cuff, the seam edge may be slightly shorter. Pin and sew it this way. The cuff has now been correctly rolled and stitched and can be applied to the

sleeve. When a woven interfacing is used, it is better to cut it on the bias. There is no need to cut away the upper seam allowance. The woven interfacing can be sewed right in with the regular seam, because it will press flat and give a sharp crease at the edge of the cuff.

Making the one-piece cuff

Cut the upper and under cuff in one piece. Fold through the center and

press. Cut the interfacing half the width of the cuff, or to the fold line. Cut away the underarm seam allowance on the interfacing. Press the cuff on the length. Pin the interfacing from the lower edge to the fold line and stitch. This stitched side becomes the under cuff.

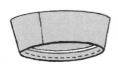

Sew up underarm seam of the cuff and make the upper cuff a little larger by taking a smaller seam at the upper section. Press open the under seam. Fold the cuff on the original fold line and press again.

Roll the cuff back with the upper cuff on the outside. Pin the open edges together—the upper edge will be a little short. Sew it this way and the roll of the cuff will be correct before it is sewed to the sleeve. (Both woven and nonwoven interfacings are applied in the same manner for this type of two-piece cuff.)

Sewing cuff to sleeve

Both the one-piece and two-piece cuffs are first sewed to the sleeve edge; then the facing is applied. The same method used for facing a sleeve can also be used for the sleeve with a cuff. Instructions for either shaped or bias facing are on page 42.

When the cuff is self-finished, the lower edges are *not* sewed together before the cuff is applied to sleeve.

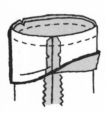

On a washable dress, the cuff can be applied entirely by machine. Pin the right side of your upper cuff to the wrong side of sleeve and stitch. Turn under the free edge of the under cuff and pin along the stitching line. Turn the cuff up over the sleeve to be sure it rolls right. Leave the outside cuff slightly longer for better roll on the finished sleeve.

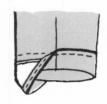

Sew pinned edge of cuff to sleeve by machine-stitch.

On a non-washable fabric, self-finish the cuff by hand. Pin the free edge of the under cuff to the right side of the sleeve and stitch. Press the seam into the cuff. Turn the sleeve right side out, then carefully roll the cuff back over the sleeve. Now, you're ready to pin the cuff to the sleeve of the garment as it will roll. Then turn sleeve inside out.

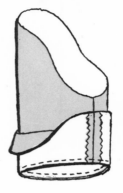
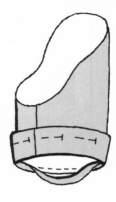

Turn under the free edge of outside cuff and slipstitch along the stitching line, and the sleeve is finished. Turning the cuff back before sewing it insures that the cuff is rolling correctly.

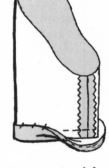

You can apply the separate cuff to a garment with a three-quarter sleeve in the same way as described above.

Finishing ¾ sleeve

Generally, the finishing on a short or a three-quarter sleeve is similar, and the same technique is used. There is one type of cuff treatment, however, that is used almost exclusively with the three-quarter sleeve.

This is the cuff cut all in one piece

with the sleeve, and finished with a separate facing. It can be a simple turned-up type of cuff, or a harder-to-make faced cuff with side opening.

Sleeve and cuff in one

The sleeve seam is sewed and pressed

open. Before you sew the facing, remember that it is always made smaller so it will fit smoothly inside the sleeve. The outer cuff is always made a little larger so it will roll correctly. This facing combines the two; it is outer cuff and inside facing in one. Here is a trick to use when sewing the seam. On the part that forms the cuff, take a more shallow seam. This

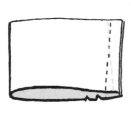

will make the cuff a bit larger, and as you sew it to the facing part of the cuff, take a deeper seam so the facing will be a little smaller.

Cut the interfacing from the facing pattern. Cut it on the bias if it is a woven fabric. Then join the interfacing seam and press it open.

Pin the interfacing to the wrong

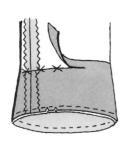

side of the sleeve. Sew it to the edge of the sleeve by machine. Trim off $5/8$ inch from the loose edge of the interfacing. Then catch-stitch interfacing to sleeve. Now pin and stitch the facing to the lower edge of the sleeve, with the right sides together. The facing forms the outer cuff and, since it was made a little larger, it will have to be eased.

Trim the seam allowance to graduated widths. Turn the facing to the

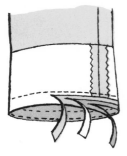
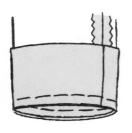

inside and baste the edge, bringing the sleeve edge in slightly. Now lightly press the sleeve.

Turn the sleeve right side out and roll the cuff back on the sleeve. Pin to hold it in the correct position. Turn the sleeve wrong side out. Turn under the facing edge and stitch. Slip-stitch it to the sleeve. The cuff is sure to roll correctly when it is sewed in place on the dress.

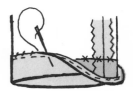

Sleeve and open cuff in one

When the sleeve is only slashed to create an open cuff, it is relatively simple to make. If the opening of the cuff is formed by the continuation of a dart or seam, it may be more complicated. Here's a simple technique used by professionals to make this type of sleeve.

Slash-type opening

Follow the same procedure as for the cuff and facing in one. Sew up the sleeve and facing as described. Follow the instructions for cutting the interfacing and sewing it to the sleeve. After you have applied the interfacing, mark the position of the slash. Run a line of machine-stitching along the marked seamline

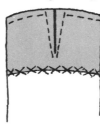
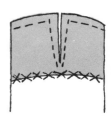

of the slash. Slash between these lines to the point of the opening.

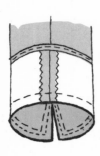

Pin the right side of the facing to the right side of the sleeve and stitch it on sleeve side. Ease the facing in slightly as you pin it. Along the slash, sew just outside the marked stitching line.

Slash the facing after it is sewed. Trim the seam allowance to graduated widths. Turn the facing to inside, and baste it close to edge, bringing the sleeve back slightly. Baste around the slash the same way and press lightly. Roll the cuff back to the right side and pin it into place. Slip-stitch the facing in place as you do on the other faced cuff.

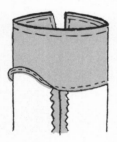
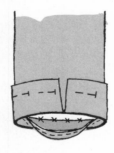

Cuff opening at seam

Whether the opening for the cuff comes on a seam or a dart, be sure to check your pattern and carefully mark the point to which you sew. Mark it on both sleeve and facing.

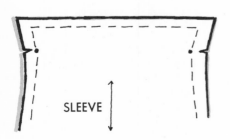

Sew up the sleeve and facing seams, and press. At the point where the cuff will open, clip into the stitching line on both sleeve and facing.

Again, make the facing slightly larger than the sleeve at the open edge, but a little smaller where it is to finish inside the sleeve.

Cut and apply the interfacing on the sleeve as you do for the cuff in one. There is no need to sew the seam on the interfacing, since it will be trimmed away, and seam edges lapped to the sleeve seam and tacked.

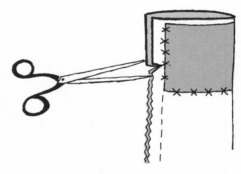

Pin the right side of the facing to the right side of the sleeve. Be sure to ease the facing as you pin. For the cuff opening, carefully match the clipped seam on the sleeve with the clipped seam on the facing. Sew the two pieces together from this point. Finish it as you do the cuff with the slash opening.

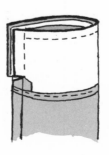
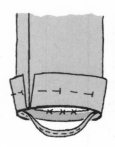

Long sleeve

You can use the same detail on the long sleeve as you do on the three-quarter sleeve. There is one finish, however, that is needed only on the long sleeve. This is the placket opening at the wrist on the tight-fitting sleeve. It's described below.

Placket

The lower end of a long sleeve is left open for about 4 inches so that your hand can easily pass through it. Use seam binding for a flat and easy-to-apply finish on this type of sleeve.

Sew seam binding to the back sleeve opening, $\frac{1}{8}$ inch from the edge of the seam. Then continue to sew around the bottom edge of the sleeve on $\frac{5}{8}$ inch seamline, and up the front opening just outside of the regular $\frac{5}{8}$-inch seamline. Next, turn

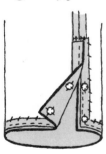

the seam binding to the inside and hem to the inside of the sleeve. Miter the corners, turn under ends, and finish. Press. Then lap the top of the back seam over the front and stitch by hand into position. Sew snaps at the sleeve opening.

Other types

Instructions for making additional types of sleeves and cuff finishes for special clothes, such as sportswear and casual clothes, are shown in other Creative Sewing Library books.

Kimono sleeve

The underarm seam of the kimono sleeve is always reinforced, since no gusset is used. Reinforcement is necessary because, to make underarm seam smooth, it must be clipped around the curve, and it could easily tear. This reinforcement can be done by machine or hand, depending on the quality

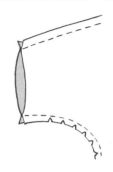

of the dress and the type of fabric. There are several methods that you can use to reinforce a sleeve. Choose the most suitable one for your garment from the following.

By machine

Fold a piece of seam binding in half on the length and press. As you sew the underarm seam, catch the binding at the same time. Make it long enough to cover the whole curve of the seam where it will be clipped. Clip the seam and press it open.

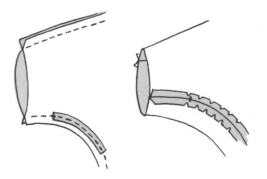

Another method is to sew the seam, clip it, and press it open. Fold the seam binding on the length and press. Baste the binding along the center of the seam on the wrong side. Turn the garment right side out and stitch

⅛ inch on either side of the seam. You can also do this with a fine zig-zag stitch, if you have this type of machine or an attachment.

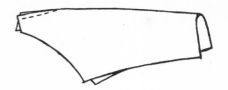

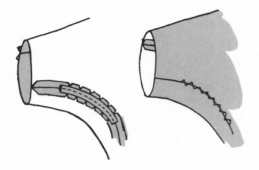

bodice pieces before sewing the underarm seam. Be sure to clip the seam at the underarm curve, then press it open. Stitch the underarm bodice and sleeve seams all in one. Press the underarm seam open. It may be neces-

By hand

Sew the side seam by machine. Clip, press open the seam. Press seam binding in half on the length. (You can use seam binding or a ¼-inch satin or taffeta ribbon.) Place the binding or ribbon in the center of the seam on the inside of the dress. Take a fine running-stitch by hand down the center, catching it to the center seam. Then do a fine hemming-stitch all around to complete the reinforcing.

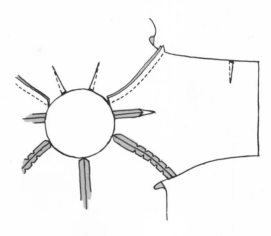

sary to clip at the underarm seam to make it lie flat and smooth.

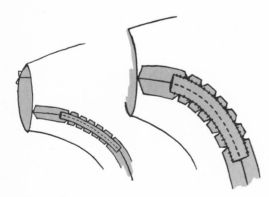

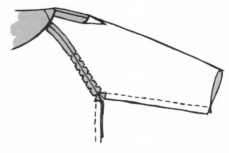

Raglan sleeve

This sleeve must be handled in a slightly different manner from most of the others. First, sew up the shoulder dart or seam, and press. Next, join the sleeve to the back and front

After you have finished and joined the bodice and sleeves, you are ready to work on the skirt. Your skirt can be completely finished before it is joined to the bodice. It's easier to handle a section of the garment at a time; the work will be neater and more professional-looking when the garment is assembled.

Finishing the skirt

The only major finishing needed on the skirt is the hem, and the pressing. There are many types of hems. Analyze the style of skirt and the fabric you are using in order to choose the correct one for your garment.

Circular hem

On a full circular skirt, never make more than a 2½-inch hem. Otherwise, it will look bulky and have too much ease. Press back the hem on the hemline mark. Measure in for the depth of hem and cut off the excess.

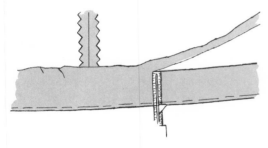

Sew around the edge of the hem by machine on the right side, close to the edge. Use a large stitch on the machine. If the skirt has gores, stitch from one seam to the other, starting the new stitching at each gore. By sewing it in this manner, you can ease in the fullness on only one gore at a time. If your circular skirt has more than six gores, run the shirring to take in two gores at a time.

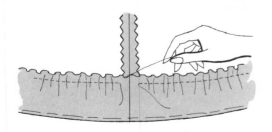

Ease in all the hem fullness so it is smooth and flat to the inside of the skirt. On the gored skirt, be sure that the seams line up correctly, one on top of the other.

Sew a seam binding on the edge of the hem and slip-stitch into place.

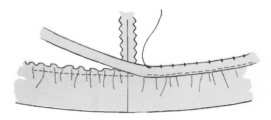

Circular hem on a sheer

Mark the hem on a sheer in the same manner as for the circular skirt, turn, press, and trim. Instead of using a seam binding on the edge, turn under ¼ inch on the hem and sew all around by machine with a large stitch.

Ease in the hem fullness so that the hem lies flat and smooth inside of the skirt. Be sure that the seams are placed one over the other. Pin into place. Slip-stitch the fold edge of the hem to the skirt.

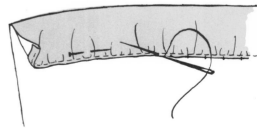

Flared skirt

Never use more than a 3-inch hem on a slightly flared skirt. Turn, press, and trim hem to desired depth. You can apply seam binding without first easing hem. Hold binding slightly taut as you stitch it to hem. Slip-stitch to skirt, making sure seamlines match. If skirt is more flared, it may be difficult to ease. Follow the method shown for a circular skirt.

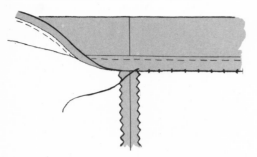

Dirndl or gathered skirt

On this type of skirt, the depth of hem depends on the fabric.

Sheer

A sheer dress looks more fashionable if the hem is from 6 to 12 inches deep. It must be carefully done to maintain the quality look which the deep hem gives. Measure, turn, and trim the hem. Press at the hemline.

Turn the edge of the hem under ¼ inch and press. Pin the hem carefully in place so all seams match. Sew the hem with a long slip-stitch.

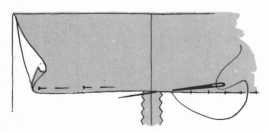

Cotton

On a cotton dress, press back, mark and trim the hem. Then turn under ¼ inch on the edge of the hem and stitch. Pin the hem into place and slip-stitch to the dress.

Remember the seams of the skirt must match when the hem is pinned.

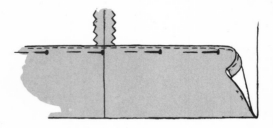

Other fabrics

Turn, press, and trim the hem in the same manner as for cotton. Then sew a seam binding to the edge of the hem before sewing it to the dress.

Pleat at the hem

This hem should be flat, but stay in pleat. Before turning the hem, press open the pleat seam to twice the

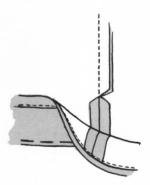

depth of the hem. Slip-stitch the hem to the skirt. Then clip to the stitching line at the top of the hem on the pleat seam to release the seam so the hem

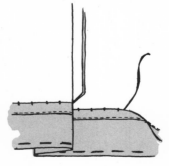

and pleat can be correctly pressed in a sharp, flat line.

Hems with facings or slits

The facing must finish back over the hem on the open-front dress. Turn up the hem and finish it according to the style of skirt and type of fabric. Slipstitch the hem to the skirt to the point where the facing laps.

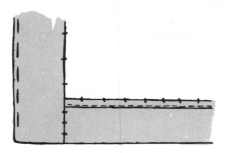

Fold the facing back over the hem and finish to the hem.

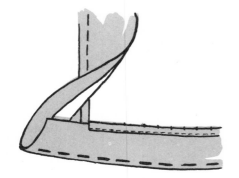

Facing and hem are cut away under the facing on heavy fabric.

Finish the slit skirt with the hems

of the slits turned back. They are sewed to the hem after the hem has been turned and pressed.

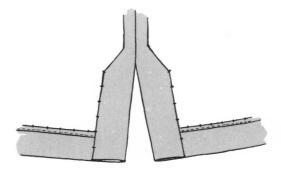

Use seam binding on the edge of the slit facings, or just turn the facings back by machine, depending on the weight of your fabric.

Lining the slit skirt

It's customary to line a slit skirt so the underslip doesn't show. Cut lining of China silk or a sheath lining, using same pattern as for skirt. Sew up lining, and then join it to skirt at waistline only. Lining hangs free inside the skirt.

In side or back of skirt, seam is left open at hem to form slit. Sew up this seam in lining. Sew patch of skirt fabric to lining under slit. It should be 8 inches wide by 2 inches deeper than slit. Hem patch in with lining.

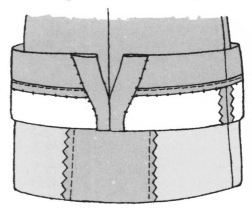

Stitched hem

Many skirt hems are now stylishly made with rows of top-stitching as a finish. This detail is usually found on rather heavy fabrics, such as tweed, double-knit jersey, linen, and heavy cottons or on woolens. It's a smart finish, but must be carefully done to avoid a homemade look to the skirt.

As quilting and trapunto are coming into fashion, stitched hems are also being done on lighter-weight fabrics, such as shantung or taffeta.

You can create this fashionable quilted effect on a skirt by using a strip of sheet cotton in the hem of the garment.

Mark and turn the skirt hem. Measure so hem is deep enough to allow for number of rows of stitching you plan to use. Trim hem to width of stitching, plus an extra ½ inch.

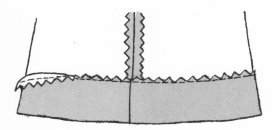

Pink the edge of the hem and stitch it close to the edge. Turn and baste hem on correct line. Press lightly. Measure and baste rows of stitching

to be used. Thread machine, using buttonhole twist or heavy-duty thread for top thread only. Be sure presser foot is adjusted to thickness of fabric, so hem will not crawl and stretch as you sew, causing it to ripple. Loosen top tension for heavier thread, so stitch won't pucker. Starting at the side seam, sew rows of stitching on the right side of the skirt.

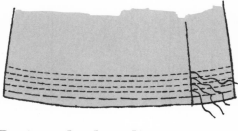

Facing the hemline

If there is not enough fabric for the hem and it must be faced, you can use self-fabric or a commercial bias to extend it.

Stitch the self-fabric or bias to the hem, right sides of the fabrics together. Allow a ¼-inch seam allowance. Press the seam open, turn under the facing fabric to form the hem on the inside. The seamline of the facing should be turned under, so the seam is not at the edge of the hem, but in about ½ inch. By doing this, the seam will not form a ridge at the edge of the skirt.

Finish the edge of the facing with a seam binding, or turn under by machine before slip-stitching to the garment. Use the finish best-suited to the facing fabric.

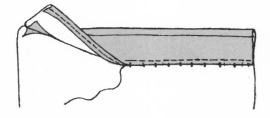

Underlining skirts and dresses

Underlining and interfacing fabrics

It's important for you to become acquainted with the variety of fabrics that can be used for interfacing and for underlining, and to learn when and how to use them correctly.

A number of commercial interfacing and underlining fabrics are available. These come in two major types —woven and nonwoven.

The nonwoven type is made by fusing fibers together. There is no grain line, so it can be cut in any direction, will not ravel, and never loses its shape. One of the nonwoven fabrics is made with a bias stretch. It also has no grain, but it is not as static as the others, and thus can be stretched in any direction. This makes it much more pliable and soft. It also retains its shape, never ravels.

The other type of commercial underlining is a woven, preshrunk fabric that has a very smooth texture. It is finished in different weights and in degrees of crispness. This type is particularly good for use in suits.

There is a type of lining fabric— the sheath lining—that is also sometimes used for underlining. Sheath linings are discussed in detail in the lining section, page 58. Some underlinings and interfacings are coated with adherent and can be pressed on.

Some of the basic fabrics, such as organdy, organza, net, taffeta, lawn, percale, cambric, muslin, can also sometimes be used as underlinings.

Where to use underlinings

The style of dress you are making and the type of fabric chosen will determine the best underlining to use. The weight and the texture of the outer fabric is an important consideration. The underlining should never impose itself on the outer fabric.

For instance, you would never use a heavy, nonwoven underlining with a soft silk print. It would make the silk look harsh, and the skirt would move and bend stiffly with the under fabric. Instead, you should select a lightweight, bias, nonwoven fabric that gives garment body, yet blends with the silk. Taffeta, organza, or a commercial woven underlining with a soft finish could also be used.

With so many different fabrics now available, it is hard to set rules. A good test is to try the outer fabric over different weights of underlinings until you find one that gives the exact texture that you want.

The style of your garment is the other determining factor. Once, when you wanted to make a tailored dress, you had to choose a firm fabric—one suitable for tailoring. Now, you can select a silk surah or any other soft fabric and, with the proper underlining, you can make it into a tailored suit. You can exercise real selectivity and imagination in choosing fabrics.

Take a look at current ready-to-wear styles and see how the designers have adapted fabrics. Lace bathing suits, chiffon suits, brocade shirt dresses, velvet slacks—there is no limit to clothes you can make when you use the under fabrics correctly.

Here are a few professional tips to keep in mind as you work with underlinings. If the upper fabric is bulky, it will tend to look bunchy when a dart is made by sewing upper and under fabric together. It will look much better if the darts are made separately in each layer of fabric, and layers are sewed together.

If an underlining is to be used in a washable garment, be sure the underlining will not shrink. It might be best to preshrink it as you would a cotton fabric. The label on a commercial underlining will tell you whether the fabric can be washed.

NOTE: When it is necessary to underline a stretchy fabric, such as jersey, crepe, or some novelty knits, always use a woven underlining. Use China silk, taffeta, or one of the more firm sheath linings that can be used as either lining or underlining.

Analyzing the style

Let's imagine, for example, that you have picked a pattern with a very full skirt. The pattern clearly indicates a bouffant look. The skirt should puff out sharply from the waist, but your fabric is too soft to give the right effect. You could put a petticoat under it, but the effect at the waistline would not be quite right.

The answer is an underlining. This can be a lightweight, nonwoven interfacing, or a crisp, woven type. The trick is in the way you make your skirt. If you want it to puff out at the waist, make up the outer skirt first. Cut the underlining from the same pattern and sew it up. Put the underlining against the wrong side of the upper skirt. Then shirr or pleat the top of the skirt (whichever the pattern shows), keeping the underlining and skirt together. This method will give the desired effect. Handle the two layers of fabric as if you were working on a single skirt layer.

By using the proper underlining, you have built the bouffant look permanently into your skirt. The non-woven underlinings never lose their shape; most of the woven ones have a crisp finish that will last the life of the garment. Your skirt will look better if the underlining is hidden, so add a lining when making any quality garment. Lining can be cut from the same pattern as the upper skirt, or it can be cut as a straight, slim underskirt. Decide which is best for the weight of fabric and type of garment.

If you cut the lining from the upper skirt pattern, sew it together as you did the skirt. Put the wrong side of the lining against the wrong side of the skirt, with the underlining between the two. Pleat or shirr all three of the thicknesses together.

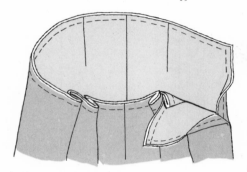

If this method of lining the skirt would make it too bulky at the waistline, use a slim, underskirt lining. Cut the lining from a pattern for a straight, fitted skirt in the correct hip size. Sew it together. Fit it into the waistline of bouffant skirt that has already been shirred or pleated. Put wrong side of lining against the wrong side of the skirt, with underlining in between. Sew it in place only at the waistline. Hem the lining and let it hang free inside skirt.

If your dress has a bell shape, an A-line, or is darted to fit the waist, but hang very full to the bottom of the hem, it must be specially made to retain this shape. To achieve it successfully, you will have to use a method that is called "mounting."

Mounting a skirt

Professional dressmakers apply an underlining by "mounting," and you can use the same technique in your own sewing. Simply cut the underlining from the same pattern pieces as the upper fabric to be mounted. Use either a nonwoven type or a crisp woven underlining in a weight suitable for the upper fabric. (If you use a nonwoven one, you can lay out the pattern pieces and then cut in any direction, regardless of grain.

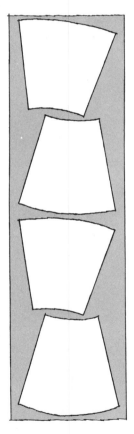

Now place the underlining to the wrong side of the upper fabric. The professional does this step at the ironing board. Press the two layers together, as you pin them carefully together. This allows for any shrinkage in either of the fabrics before the skirt or dress is finally assembled.

Place skirt and underlining on the ironing board, with the underlining on top. Pin along one side and across the top, holding underlining and skirt fabric together. Press lightly. Put

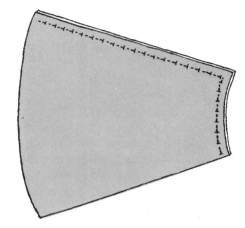

several pins down the center of the skirt panel to hold the two layers together. Roll the pinned side over so that the skirt fabric is on top. Slide skirt piece over on the board and pin remaining side seam of skirt.

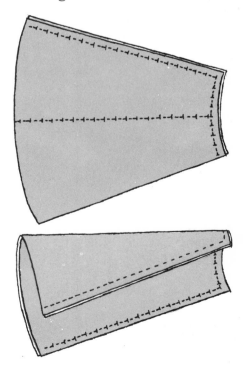

In this way the underlining is pinned exactly as it will fit inside the skirt. As the skirt rolls around the contour of the figure, the outside fabric layer should be slightly larger than the under layer. This is allowed for by rolling the outside fabric over the under fabric as you pin them. When you pin the second side of the skirt seam, you will notice that the underlining now extends a little beyond the edge of the skirt fabric. This is correct. When the skirt is worn, the underlining will lie smooth and flat and will not buckle under the upper fabric. The heavier the upper fabric, the more necessary this is. The amount is automatically controlled if it is rolled and then pinned just as the pieces are pressed. Leave the hem unpinned.

Sew the upper fabric and underlining together all around by machine, except at the hem. *Never stitch the hem edges together*. Use a long stitch and sew about ¼ inch in from the edge. You can sew the pinned edges, which is fast and accurate, or you can baste the edges together and then stitch by machine. Care is necessary, not because you stitch from either pins or basting, but because of the direction in which you stitch.

On a gored skirt, for example, it would be easiest to stitch up one side, then across the top, and down the

Wrong

other side. There is a tendency for the upper fabric to crawl, however, no matter how carefully you stitch. This could cause the whole panel to twist. The right-hand side would push up as you sewed, and the left-hand side would shift down, so that the upper surface would be twisted.

Instead, sew up first one side and then across the top. Then start at the hem and sew up the other side. With

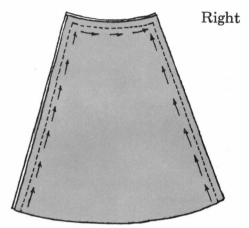

Right

this method, if the fabric shifts, it will do so all in the same direction and it will not twist. Try stitching the upper fabric and the underlining together with a test sample to see which side has the least tendency to crawl. Nonwoven underlinings shift very little, so the underlining would usually be placed on top. Woven underlinings vary as to firmness and crispness, so test them first. If the upper fabric is firm, it may be best to sew with it on top. If you sew it without testing and find excessive crawling in the fabric on top, turn it over and try the other side.

It's always safer to make pattern markings after the fabric is mounted. Re-lay the pattern on the underlining side and mark for inside sewing, such as darts, tucks, clipping corners or gussets. For the outer detail, such as pockets, mark directly from the pattern, placed on the upper fabric. Use these techniques for sewing under-linings in all garments.

Sewing darts

There is a special way to sew darts when underlinings are used. Always sew through the center of the dart to hold the two layers of fabric together. Then you can sew the darts. The

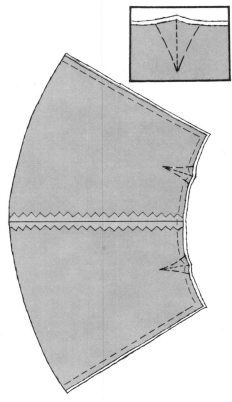

stitching that holds upper fabric and underlining together can be used as an outline stitch where special seaming is indicated on a pattern. For example, if a gusset is used in the dress bodice, a line on the pattern piece indicates where and how the gusset is to be inserted. Mark the underlining for the gusset. Sew around bodice piece in usual way to join upper and under fabrics. When you reach the point where the gusset goes, adjust ma-

chine to a small stitch. Carefully sew around gusset markings. This indicates sewing line, and small stitch helps reinforce the corner. This same

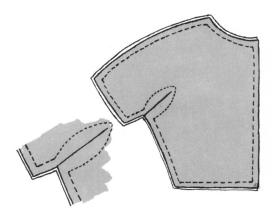

technique also is helpful in the other parts of the garment, where stitching, shaping, or additional reinforcing is required.

Underlining a straight skirt

A straight skirt is rarely underlined. Usually, the lining is adequate. It is simply dropped into the skirt and is designed to hang free.

Some women prefer to mount a straight skirt on a silk lining because it is easier to hem to a lining without showing a hemming mark on the right side. Unfortunately, the seams appear to pucker when a skirt is mounted on a lining fabric. If the fabric of the skirt is spongy or stretchy, one that is likely to lose its shape, it should be mounted—but it should be mounted only on an under-lining fabric. Use a woven underlining for this type of upper fabric. Cut the underlining from the same skirt pattern and mount it, then pin, and sew it as is shown on page 56. After the skirt is sewed together, it should be lined with a soft sheath lining. Use fabric such as China silk.

Lining dresses and skirts

A quality dress should almost always be lined, whether or not it has been underlined. Decide whether your dress will be washed or dry cleaned, and be sure to use a washable lining in a washable dress. (Casual cottons and sport clothes are seldom lined; special parts can be underlined.)

China silk is particularly good for linings. It is so soft that, even if the lining is made slightly larger than the dress, no mark or wrinkle will show on the right side. It is particularly good for lining fabrics like jersey that have a tendency to cling and need a lining for a smooth look. (Don't confuse jersey with double-knit fabrics. The double-knits do *not* need to be lined, unless you wish to give a garment added quality.)

Other linings, generally called sheath linings, resemble China silk but are made of fiber blends. Though these fabrics are not as soft or fine as China silk, they still work very well for linings. There are so many lining fabrics available that it's a good idea to check a number of them before you decide which to buy. Some can also be used as underlinings.

Never line a dress with fabric that has any roughness to its texture. A lining is meant to make a dress hang better and fit more smoothly. If the lining is rough, it will cling to the inside of the dress and create wrinkles. Be sure your lining fabric is really suitable for the individual job.

Lining a shift dress

The lining of a shift is made to hang free inside the dress. It is attached at armholes, neckline, and along the zipper. The hem is made separately in the dress and the lining. Cut the lining from the same pattern as the dress. Cut it 1 inch shorter at the hem. Sew up all the darts and seams, and press carefully.

Put the wrong side of the lining against the wrong side of the dress and pin carefully all around armholes and neckline. Lap the lining over the zipper tape and pin into place. Be

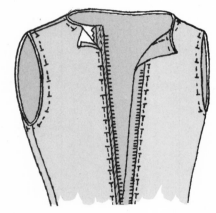

sure the lining fits smoothly inside the dress. Check seams and darts of the lining against the seams and darts of the dress. Lining may seem too full on a dress with a back zipper; this only occurs when not enough of the lining has been turned under when you lapped it over the zipper.

Stitch lining into place around the neck and armholes. Pin the armhole and neckline facing into place and stitch. (For dress with sleeves, see next page.) Trim and clip neck and armhole seam all around. Turn the facings to the inside, baste around edges, press lightly and carefully.

To pin facing into place for finishing, place the armhole and neckline over a tailor's mitt on your sleeve board. Pin carefully so facings fit smoothly to shape and curve of the

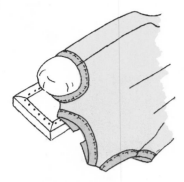

armhole and neck. Finish it with a slip-stitch to the lining only. None of hand-stitching shows on the right side. Slip-stitch lining to zipper tape along the edge. Then do a running-stitch. This catches the lining to the zipper tape about $\frac{1}{4}$ inch from the first stitch. This prevents the lining from rolling into the chain of the zipper and becoming snagged.

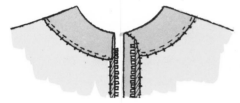

Sleeves

Line a short sleeve, if you choose, but a longer dress sleeve is seldom lined unless the fabric irritates the skin. Sew the dress lining to the armhole first, and set the sleeve into the armhole, catching the lining and dress in one seam. If the sleeve is lined, sew the lining and sleeve cap together, ease and set sleeve into armhole, catching both lining and sleeve in one stitching. For a really elegant look, the sleeve can be set into the armhole separately and the sleeve lining lapped over the seam and then slip-stitched by hand.

Lining a skirt

With the exception of some cottons,

skirts are nearly always lined, no matter what the fabric.

Cut the lining from the same pattern as the skirt. Make the lining up separately. Before you finish the top of the skirt, drop the lining into it; place inside of lining against inside of skirt. Pin skirt and lining together all around the waistline.

Insert zipper and apply the waistband. Make hems separately in skirt and lining. The hem on the outer skirt is turned to the inside; the lining hem of the skirt will be turned to the side that shows the raw seams.

Trimming detail

Often the trimming detail on a dress or suit consists of a decorative banding or design that is applied after the garment is made. It's important that this trim be perfectly shaped and, if used in pairs, that the pieces match exactly. Trim can be sewed either by hand or by machine, depending on how and where used.

Nonwoven underlining is ideal for this kind of detail. Those with an adherent are easiest to use. The underlining is applied to the under side of the upper fabric, so first be sure that it can be applied without affecting the upper one. *Always test the upper fabric before using.* Heavier or thicker fabrics, such as wool or some cottons, are usually safe, but on a thin silk, for example, you may get a reaction to the adherent. Sometimes a piece of organza, used between the underlining and the silk, will prevent marking. *If there is any reaction, however, it is safer to use a plain nonwoven underlining and catch-stitch it in place.*

View 1

This style has a scroll-shaped banding used as trim at the neckline. To make it, cut the shaped banding to the finished size in a nonwoven underlining. Then cut the trim in fabric, allowing seam allowances. Place the underlining to the wrong side of the upper fabric with the seam allowances extending all around, and press in place. (If non-adherent underlining is used, catch-stitch it in place.) Clip in on the seam allowance all around and turn it back over the underlining. Baste carefully all around the trim. The cut edge of the under-

lining acts as a guide line in shap-

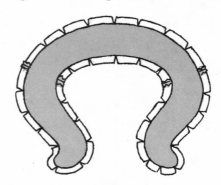

ing it. Press lightly. Apply this trim by hand for a fine dress detail.

View 2

A tab trim is used on this jacket to simulate pockets and form belt loops. Bands are sewed flat to the jacket with just the ends faced and turned back to form the loop.

Cut band and facing piece of the upper fabric. Cut underlining to the finished size, and press it to the wrong side of the upper fabric. Sew facing to the band, right sides together. Turn facing to the wrong side. Baste around the trimming band, shaping the point and turning back the seam allowances. Press lightly.

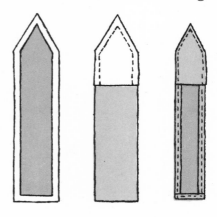

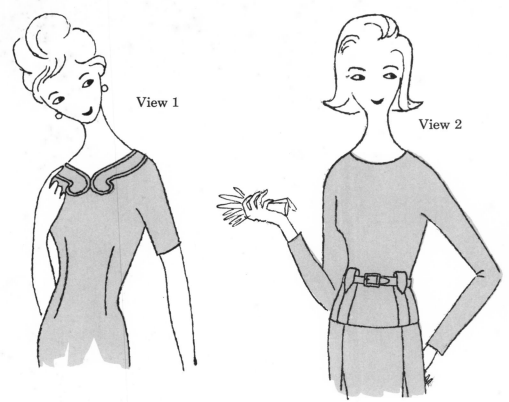

View 1

View 2

Sew to the suit by hand. Turn back the point and tack to form belt loop.

View 3

This waist trim is applied to a shift dress. It's designed to simulate a high, shaped waistline detail.

Cut the band from the upper fabric, adding seam allowances. Cut the underlining to the finished size, and press to wrong side of trimming band. Clip and turn the seam allowance

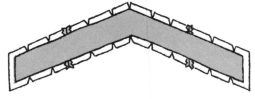

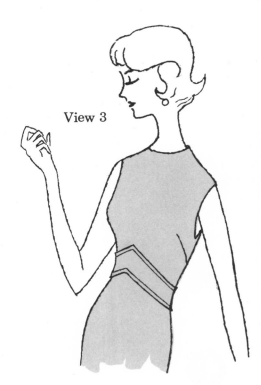

View 3

and baste all around. Then press lightly. Pin the band into place on the dress and stitch it in place by machine about $\frac{1}{2}$ inch in from edge.

INDEX